Prophets:
Preachers for God

TOM McMINN • ILLUSTRATED BY H. DON FIELDS

BROADMAN PRESS
Nashville, Tennessee

4242-50
ISBN: 0-8054-4250-2

Dewey Decimal Classification: J221.92
Subject heading: PROPHETS

Printed in the United States of America.

Contents

Elisha, the Traveling Prophet

Elisha remembered how his teacher Elijah had entrusted him with God's work. Elisha knew he would be God's spokesman to Israel. The day by the Jordan River when Elijah was taken in a whirlwind to heaven, Elisha began to carry on the work of the Lord.

Elisha knew God would use him in a special way. He would train helpers to carry on the schools of the prophets which

Elijah had started. Elisha traveled to
Gilgal, Bethel, and Jericho where the
schools were located. He wanted to visit
these schools to encourage the sons of the
prophets in their work. They knew that
Elisha was God's spokesman.

Elisha helped people in many ways. One
day he entered a city and made plans to
stay with a poor widow.

The widow told Elisha that she owed
money to the man who owned the house
she lived in. And the man wanted his

money. The widow told Elisha the man would sell her two sons into slavery to get his money.

Elisha wanted to help the widow. He asked, "Tell me what you have in the house."

The widow said, "I have some furniture and a small jar of oil."

Elisha thought for a moment. Then he said, "Go, bring me as many jars as you can find."

The widow went to many of her friends and neighbors and borrowed jars. She returned to her house. She placed all the jars by Elisha.

Then Elisha spoke to the widow, "Pour oil from your jar into all the jars."

The widow did as Elisha instructed. She was able to fill all the jars with oil. She told Elisha what had happened. Elisha said: "Sell the oil and pay the man who owns the house. There will be enough money left to live on."

Elisha helped many people. He helped a woman of Shunem who was kind to him.

He helped an enemy captain named Naaman get well from a skin disease. And, during a famine in Gilgal, Elisha helped his servant prepare good food for the sons of the prophets.

God protected Elisha and provided for him, even from kings. One of these kings was the king of Syria.

The king of Syria wanted Israel to
belong to him. But each time he tried to
capture a city, he failed. The cities of Israel
were well guarded. How did Jehoram,
king of Israel, always know when and
where the Syrian army was going to attack?
The king of Syria thought someone was
telling Jehoram his secret plans.

8

One day the king of Syria told his soldiers, "Find the person who tells secret plans to my enemy Jehoram of Israel."

After a time the soldiers reported, "It is Elisha who tells Jehoram your plans."

"Elisha must be captured," the Syrian king said. He sent his army to find Elisha.

The army of Syria surrounded the town of Dothan where Elisha lived. Elisha's servant ran to warn Elisha about the approaching army. "What are we going to do?" the servant asked Elisha, "Where can we hide? Come, we must leave now."

Elisha said: "Don't be afraid. There are more with us than with the army of Syria."

This was hard for the servant to

understand. The army had many men.

Elisha said, "God, let my servant see what I see." The servant saw horses and chariots of fire on the mountains. Now the servant knew God was going to protect Elisha. The servant was not afraid of the army of Syria any longer.

As the army of Syria approached Dothan, the soldiers became blind.

Elisha met the soldiers and said: "Follow me. I will take you to the man you want."

Elisha led the blind soldiers away from Dothan into the city of Samaria. Inside the city gates Elisha prayed, "God, open the eyes of these men so they can see."

When the men opened their eyes and saw where they were, they became afraid. Samaria was the city where King Jehoram lived.

King Jehoram saw the enemy army. He

11

was surprised to see them in the city. Jehoram asked Elisha, "What shall I do with these men? Shall I kill them?"

"No," answered Elisha. "They are hungry. Feed them and send them on their way."

Jehoram respected Elisha as God's spokesman. He obeyed the words of Elisha and fed the soldiers of Syria. Then he let the army of Syria return to their own land.

Never again did the people of Syria try to harm Elisha. Elisha continued traveling throughout the land. He taught and encouraged the people to remain faithful to God. He helped the people learn that God will provide for their needs.

Thinkback: God used special people in special ways. He used Elisha to help many people.

Can you remember ways God helped Elisha? Can you remember ways Elisha helped others?

God helps you as you live each day. Can you think of ways God helps you?

A Special Assignment for Amos

Amos sat by the side of the main road
entering Tekoa, his hometown. He
watched caravans returning from the
seacoasts carrying goods to merchants.
Sometimes he heard what the travelers
said about other towns and places.

Amos thought of visiting some of the

places he heard about. Amos was a herdsman. The only places he visited were wool markets and places where he could sell the sycamore fruit he harvested.

Tekoa was in Judah. The king of Judah was Uzziah. Amos knew that when Solomon was king there had only been one kingdom. The twelve tribes had separated after Solomon's death. Now there were two kingdoms called Israel and Judah.

Just as God called Elisha to be his spokesman, he called Amos to leave his home in Judah to carry a message to Israel. God wanted Amos to tell the people of Israel about his judgment against them because of their unfaithfulness.

Amos began his journey to Israel. He knew God was with him. He left Tekoa and traveled north to Bethel. Bethel was the chief religious center for Israel. Bethel was where King Jeroboam of Israel worshiped.

When he got to Bethel, Amos noticed there was a celebration going on. King Jeroboam had ended a very long war. Everyone in Israel was happy.

14

Amos thought this was a good time to speak God's words. He began preaching in the streets, telling the people about what God was going to do.

"Hear what God says against you, Israel! You are the only family he has known throughout the earth. Because he knows you so well, he is going to punish you for your wrongdoings. Turn to God, and you shall live. Seek good, not evil and live."

As Amos continued preaching, a

15

religious procession came near. In the procession was Amaziah, the priest of Bethel. Amaziah was curious about the crowd and what was happening.

Amos continued: "The Lord said he would not come this way again. He said he would be against the house of King Jeroboam."

People gathered closer around Amos. They wanted to hear every word.

The statements of Amos and the interest of the crowd listening to Amos troubled Amaziah. Amaziah felt that God talked through him, not this street preacher from Judah.

When Amos said a sword would be raised against King Jeroboam, Amaziah became angry. He went to Jeroboam and said: "Amos is a traitor. He talks of killing the king. These words of Amos are not good for the people to hear while they are celebrating a victory."

Amaziah ended his plea before the king by saying, "Amos also said King Jeroboam would die by the sword and that the people

16

of Israel will be led away as captives."

After telling the king all Amos had said, Amaziah returned to the streets of Bethel to find Amos. He had the authority of the king in the words he would tell Amos.

Amaziah found Amos preaching again. He interrupted Amos' sermon. "Amos, return to Judah," said Amaziah. "Preach in Judah all you want. Do not return to Bethel," warned Amaziah.

Amos answered Amaziah, saying, "I am

17

not a preacher. I am a herdsman who gathers sycamore fruit. God talked to me as I took care of my flock. He told me to come to Israel. He said to tell the people of Israel his decision. I have done what God told me to do."

Amos' mission to Bethel was over. God only told Amos to go and to tell. Amos left Bethel. He visited other cities of Israel, telling them what God was going to do.

Thinkback: God used Amos in a special way. What did Amos do for God?

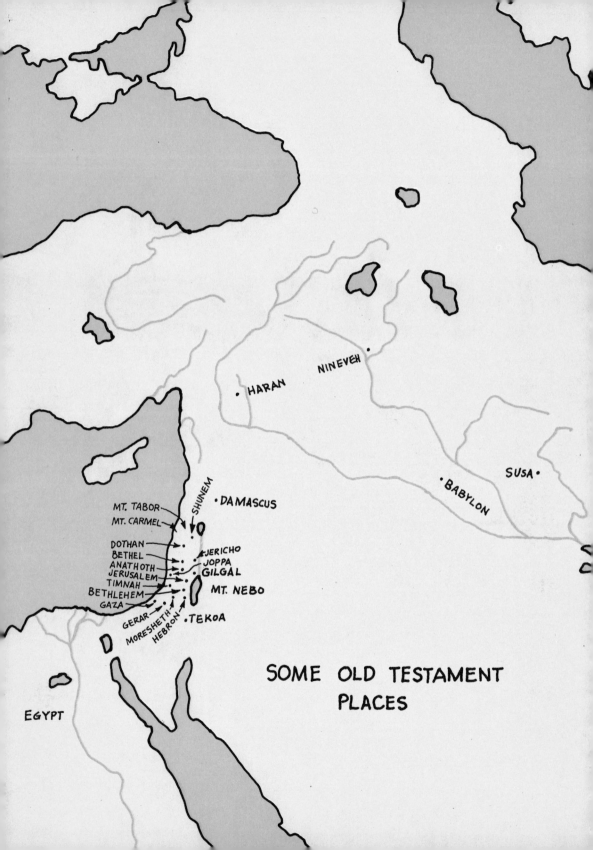

MT. TABOR
MT. CARMEL
SHUNEM
• DAMASCUS

DOTHAN
BETHEL
ANATHOTH
JERUSALEM
TIMNAH
BETHLEHEM
GAZA
GERAR
MORESHETH
HEBRON

• JERICHO
• JOPPA
GILGAL
MT. NEBO

• TEKOA

HARAN

NINEVEH

SUSA •

• BABYLON

EGYPT

SOME OLD TESTAMENT
PLACES

Jeremiah Warns the People About Captivity

Jeremiah was sad. He was leaving his hometown of Anathoth.

As Jeremiah grew, he saw that the people were not worshiping God as they should. He was troubled. Jeremiah knew the people were wrong.

God told Jeremiah to tell the people to be faithful to God and to obey his laws. Jeremiah had tried to tell his family and friends in Anathoth. He had told them, "God will punish you if you do not change your ways."

But the people would not listen. They ignored Jeremiah.

Jeremiah finished his packing and left Anathoth. He started on his way to Jerusalem. Jeremiah thought about what he would do in Jerusalem. Jeremiah knew he would tell the people in Jerusalem about God's warning.

The people in Jerusalem did not believe Jeremiah. They even grew tired of hearing

Jeremiah talk.

One day the people asked King Jehoiakim to keep Jeremiah away from the Temple.

Jeremiah was sad that he could not talk with the people at the Temple. God still wanted to warn the people. So God said to Jeremiah, "Write my words on a scroll."

Baruch was a scribe who helped

Jeremiah. Jeremiah asked Baruch to write God's words and read the scroll to the people.

Baruch did as Jeremiah asked. He went to the Temple and read the words.

After hearing the words at the Temple, the princes demanded, "Baruch, give us the scroll!"

The princes took the scroll to the king.

They read the words. The king was angry.
He cut the scroll into pieces and threw the
pieces into a fire. Then he commanded,
"Bring Jeremiah and Baruch to me."
Jeremiah and Baruch were warned.

24

They hid from the king. They heard how the king had destroyed the scroll. They wanted to write God's words on another scroll. Jeremiah wanted the people, especially the king, to believe God would punish all the people.

For many years Jeremiah continued to warn the people about being captured by their enemies the Babylonians.

A new king ruled in Judah. His name was Zedekiah. Jeremiah told king Zedekiah about the captivity. The king was troubled, but he refused to hurt Jeremiah because he was a prophet.

Jeremiah told King Zedekiah, "Even you will be captured by the Babylonians."

The princes begged the king, saying, "Jeremiah is a traitor. He must die."

But the king respected Jeremiah.

When the princes saw that the king was not going to do anything about Jeremiah, they decided to put Jeremiah in prison.

They took Jeremiah to an old well in the

middle of the prison yard. There was no water in the well, but the bottom was muddy. They used ropes to lower Jeremiah into the well.

The well was very uncomfortable for Jeremiah. He had no food or water. Jeremiah thought he would die. No one seemed to care about him.

But someone did care. A man named Ebedmelech, a servant in the palace, felt sorry for Jeremiah. He could not see why a prophet of God was treated this way. Ebedmelech went to see the king.

"King Zedekiah," he said, "Jeremiah, the prophet of God, is being treated badly. He will die if you do not help him."

King Zedekiah became afraid when he heard about Jeremiah. He spoke to his guards and said, "Hurry! Get Jeremiah out of the well before he dies."

Ebedmelech led the men to the well. He called down to Jeremiah. "We are your friends, Jeremiah. We have come to get you out. Take these rags and put them under your arms. The rags will keep the ropes from hurting your arms."

Ebedmelech and the king's men pulled Jeremiah out of the well. Jeremiah thanked his new friend for helping him.

Ebedmelech said, "I am glad to help a prophet who is not afraid to say what God tells him to say, even if it causes him to be hurt."

Jeremiah was kept in the courtyard of the prison. He was treated kindly, but he could not walk through the city or talk to the people.

When Nebuchadnezzar, the king of Babylon, attacked Jerusalem, Jeremiah was given the choice of remaining in Jerusalem or going to Babylon. He chose to stay in Jerusalem. He knew God had more for him to do. He felt sad for the people being led away into captivity. Jeremiah wrote letters to encourage them in a strange land.

Years later Jeremiah traveled to Egypt with people from Jerusalem. He

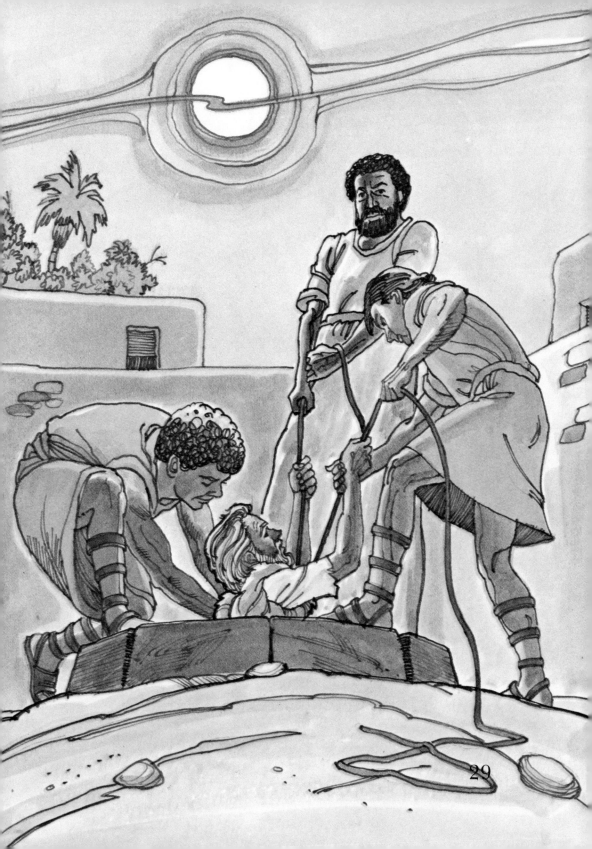

continued to encourage people until his death in Egypt.

Thinkback: Jeremiah left his hometown of Anathoth to preach for God in Jerusalem.

Do you remember the words of God which Jeremiah spoke to the people of Jerusalem?

30

Jonah's Mission to a Foreign Country

God loves all people. He wants people to know about his love and to love him. God asked a man named Jonah to go on a special mission to a foreign country. He wanted Jonah to tell the people of Nineveh about his love.

God said: "Jonah, go to the city of Nineveh. Tell the people I do not like their lying, stealing, cheating, and killing. Tell the people to change the way they live."

Jonah did not want to go to Nineveh. Nineveh was an enemy city. Jonah was afraid the people of Nineveh would hurt him if he told them to change the way they lived.

Jonah did not know what to do. He did not want to make God angry. He thought, "I will go where God cannot find me."

So Jonah hurried to the seacoast town of Joppa. He bought a ticket for the city of Tarshish.

As the boat left Joppa, Jonah felt safe

and lay down to rest.

As the boat sailed out to sea, the wind became stronger and stronger. Big waves came over the sides of the boat. Soon there was a storm.

The sailors were afraid. It was hard to keep the boat steady with the strong wind. The sailors threw things overboard to make it easier to sail the boat. They were upset to find Jonah sleeping. The sailors decided Jonah was to blame for the bad weather.

Jonah showed courage by telling the sailors he was running away from his God. The sailors were afraid of Jonah's God. They threw Jonah overboard.

In the time that followed, Jonah learned that no one can run or hide from God. Finally, Jonah decided to go to Nineveh.

As Jonah entered Nineveh, he began telling the people, "You have forty days to live. God will destroy Nineveh because of

its wickedness."

The people realized Jonah was a great prophet. They felt that God was speaking through Jonah. The people told the king.

The king ordered all the people to pray to God for forgiveness. He also commanded the people to not eat or drink until God forgave them.

To show his sincerity, the king took off his fine robe and put on a shabby robe. Then he sat in a pile of ashes and prayed to God.

Because of what the people of Nineveh did, God told Jonah he was not going to destroy the city. Jonah was unhappy with

what God said. He thought the people of
Nineveh would laugh at him. They would
say he was not a good prophet.

Jonah felt sorry for himself. He left the
city. Outside of the city, he sat down to see
what would happen. The day became very
hot. So, using sticks, Jonah built a shelter
to shade himself from the hot sun.

While Jonah rested, God made a vine to

grow and cover Jonah's shelter. Jonah was glad about the vine. The vine made his shelter cooler.

God wanted Jonah to learn something. God sent a worm to eat the stem of the vine. The vine died.

God caused the wind from the east to blow. The wind made Jonah hotter.

Now Jonah was ready to learn a very important truth from God.

God asked, "Jonah, are you sad about the vine?"

"Yes," answered Jonah.

"You are sorry a vine died?" asked God. "How can you be sorry for a plant you only knew one day? How do you think I feel about the people of Nineveh? Do you think I want them to die?"

Jonah realized God was right. Jonah had been thinking about himself, not the people of Nineveh. He learned that God loves all people. Jonah realized that people could only know God's love if people like himself were brave enough to tell them.

Thinkback: Jonah was not happy when God wanted him to go to a foreign city. Because he was unhappy, Jonah ran away from God. What great truth did Jonah learn when he tried to run away from God? What did he learn by going to Nineveh?

Micah Helps and Encourages People

The people of Judah were sad. For many years they had been told what to do and how to worship by the Assyrians. The Assyrian army had conquered the nation of Judah. The people of Judah had to pay taxes to the Assyrians. The Assyrians appointed some men in Judah to collect the taxes. If the men of Judah did not collect the taxes, the Assyrians collected more taxes from those men. This caused the men of Judah who collected taxes to be mean and hateful toward others in their country.

During these hard times some people in Judah were thrown out of their homes. Some people were made slaves.

Micah, the prophet, had shown courage several times. He had spoken against the treatment of people. He said it was unfair.

Micah lived in the town of Moresheth. It was about twenty-five miles from the capital of Judah, Jerusalem. Micah had many friends in Moresheth. Some of his friends were treated badly.

One hot day in spring, Micah sat by the well at the city gate. He had stopped to get a cool drink of water.

Micah thought of the hard times. He remembered he had warned the people about the way they lived. Micah remembered another prophet named Isaiah. Isaiah had also warned the people.

"Why was it hard for the people to understand?" Micah thought.

Micah decided it was time to tell the people again that God was displeased with what was happening.

As he walked through the gate of the city, Micah saw a woman and her children being pushed out of a house. He hurried to get closer. He wanted to find out what was happening. As he got near the house, he saw the woman was crying.

"Please do not treat me like this. This house and the things in it are all we own since my husband died. I do not have anything else," cried the woman.

"Please leave my mother alone!" one of her children shouted.

One man continued to hold the woman while other men went in and out of the house taking what they wanted. The soldiers and a crowd of people watched.

Micah pushed his way through the crowd. He tried to help the woman.

"Let this woman go," said Micah. "She has not done anything to bother anyone."

The man pushed Micah out of the way.

42

Micah fell to the ground.

Finally the man holding the woman said: "If you had given me the taxes you owe, you could have saved yourself all this trouble. We will be back. Have your taxes or you and your family will have to move."

As the man left, Micah went to the woman. "I am sorry that happened. Is there anything I can do to help you?"

"No," said the woman. "My children will help me put things away. Thank you for

43

your kindness."

The woman and her children began to pick things up in their yard. Micah turned and noticed the crowd of people who had gathered. "Here is an opportunity to talk to the people," he thought.

"God is not pleased with the way we live," said Micah. "Many of us are not following the law of Moses. The Assyrians have forced the worship of their gods on us. But we must remain faithful to the teachings of the Lord God."

The crowd of people began talking among themselves.

"Micah should be careful," said one man.

"He sure does have courage to say these things to us," said a woman.

"God wants us to remain faithful to his ways. When we follow God's laws, we will treat each other better. There will be no need to throw people out of their homes," continued Micah.

Some of the people in the crowd were interrupted by a group of diplomats from Jerusalem. The diplomats, seeing the crowd gathered, shouted, "Come, hear what good thing King Hezekiah has done."

The people turned from Micah to listen.

One of the diplomats stepped forward
and said, "King Hezekiah has opened the
doors of the Temple. Again, the people of
Judah may enter to worship as their
fathers did years ago."

God was using King Hezekiah to bring
the people back to a right worship of God.

Micah reminded the people that there
would be a hard time of captivity because
of the unfaithfulness of the people. He
also said that God was going to do
something great for his people.

"God will deliver his people from hard
times. He will send a deliverer who will set

up a new kingdom," said Micah. "The deliverer will be born in the town of Bethlehem. But remember what God requires of each person. God wants each person to be fair and to love others. God wants people to be willing to help each other. He expects each person to be faithful to God and to obey his laws."

Micah continued to remind the people about God's promise for a deliverer. He wanted the people to realize their need to ask God for his forgiveness. Micah felt God had not forgotten his people.

Thinkback: Micah lived in difficult times for God's people. God used Micah to tell his people about a very special promise. Do you remember what God's promise was about?

47

Reflections

God used spokesmen called prophets in a special way. He wanted all people to know he loved them and would provide for them if they remained faithful to him and obeyed his laws.

Do you remember the places mentioned in the stories? Do you remember what each prophet told the people?

Find on the map the places mentioned in the stories.

This chart will help you remember each prophet and his message to people.

Elisha	God will provide for our needs
Amos	Seek good, not evil
Jeremiah	Be faithful to God and obey his laws
Jonah	God's love is for all people
Micah	God will provide a deliverer